Kimberly & John Kotzian

Birds AND Beacons
OF MICHIGAN

SCHIFFER
PUBLISHING
®
4880 Lower Valley Road • Atglen, PA 19310

Copyright © 2020 by Kimberly Kotzian and John Kotzian

Library of Congress Control Number: 2019947347

All rights reserved. No part of this work may be reproduced or used in any form or by any means—graphic, electronic, or mechanical, including photocopying or information storage and retrieval systems—without written permission from the publisher.

The scanning, uploading, and distribution of this book or any part thereof via the Internet or any other means without the permission of the publisher is illegal and punishable by law. Please purchase only authorized editions and do not participate in or encourage the electronic piracy of copyrighted materials.

"Schiffer," "Schiffer Publishing, Ltd.," and the pen and inkwell logo are registered trademarks of Schiffer Publishing, Ltd.

Cover design by RoS
Type set in Archer OTF/GeoSlab 703

ISBN: 978-0-7643-5926-2
Printed in China

Published by Schiffer Publishing, Ltd.
4880 Lower Valley Road
Atglen, PA 19310
Phone: (610) 593-1777; Fax: (610) 593-2002
E-mail: Info@schifferbooks.com
Web: www.schifferbooks.com

For our complete selection of fine books on this and related subjects, please visit our website at www.schifferbooks.com. You may also write for a free catalog.

Schiffer Publishing's titles are available at special discounts for bulk purchases for sales promotions or premiums. Special editions, including personalized covers, corporate imprints, and excerpts, can be created in large quantities for special needs. For more information, contact the publisher.

We are always looking for people to write books on new and related subjects. If you have an idea for a book, please contact us at proposals@schifferbooks.com.

In loving memory of Terry Pepper—
dedicated preservationist, passionate
historian, nature lover, and generous friend.

Acknowledgments

Kimberly and John would like to thank the following people for their support in making this book possible:

Debby and Billie Smith, Pam and John Kotzian, Matt and Catarina Edison, Lloyd and Brenna Kaufman, Paul DeLisle, Russ Stebbins, John Galluzzo, Terry Pepper, Kraig Anderson, Fred Stonehouse, Bruce Lynn, Nick Korstad, Robert Wiltse, Peter Manting, Grace Truman, Jaimee Tourangeau, John Krueger, Chris Williams, Buzz Hoerr, Ron St. Germain, Jonathon Wuepper, Scott Jennex, Heather Good, Pete Schiffer, Cheryl Weber, and Carey Massimini.

Kimberly and John would also like to thank the following groups and organizations for their contributions to birding, conservation, and lighthouse history and preservation:

American Birding Association, Mich Listers (Facebook group), Birding Michigan (Facebook group), Michigan Audubon Society, Great Lakes Lighthouse Keepers Association, Michigan Lighthouse Alliance, and Michigan Lighthouse Conservancy.

Contents

Introduction

With more than 3,000 miles of coastline (second only to Alaska) and a total area of over 96,000 square miles, Michigan is a jewel for those of us who love nature and all its bounty. We are such people. Kimberly's passion is birding (Michigan has a recorded count of 450 species), while John's is Great Lakes maritime history, which includes Michigan's 129 lighthouses (the most of any state in the union). Our passions rubbed off on each other, and soon we were traveling the state of Michigan searching for birds, setting a goal to see every Michigan lighthouse.

It was on these travels that Kimberly noticed a pattern emerging. The locations of these treasured lights matched up with some of the most productive birding sites in Michigan. The same points and islands where beacons were erected to warn sailors of navigation hazards are a natural place for our avian friends, weary from a long flight, to rest and refuel before continuing their migration. These locations offer sheltered bays, coastal marshes, mudflats, and forests that are well suited to waterfowl, shorebirds, raptors, passerines, and others.

We believe this book will bring joy both to birdwatchers and lighthouse enthusiasts, and hope it encourages the conservation of our historical and natural wonders.

Lake Huron

Tawas Point Lighthouse

Tawas Point, a naturally formed sand spit that stretches out into Lake Huron, has been described by some as the Cape Cod of the Midwest. The point itself, formed by current, wind, and wave, arcs out from the mainland, separating the northern end of Saginaw Bay from the larger body of Lake Huron, and forms the natural harbor, Tawas Bay. Tawas State Park's roughly 220 acres encompass this point, providing easy public access to the Victorian-era lighthouse and excellent birding opportunities there.

The Tawas Point Lighthouse is the second lighthouse built on the point. Before 1850, mariners attempting to enter Saginaw Bay from Lake Huron had trouble seeing the end of the point at night and in heavy weather. By 1850, the federal government approved funds to build a lighthouse on Tawas Point. Construction of the first light began in 1852 and was completed in 1853.

This first beacon marked Tawas Point for roughly twenty years before a replacement was needed. The natural forces that had originally formed Tawas Point had continued to shape the point, extending it nearly another mile out into Saginaw Bay. What's more, the lighthouse was deteriorating due to poor construction. With mariners calling for a new beacon, in 1875 funds were approved for a new lighthouse. Construction began in the summer of 1876, and the light was lit in time for the 1877 shipping season. The second lighthouse, at 67 feet tall, remains the most iconic feature of Tawas State Park.

Tawas Point's unique geography makes it a natural resting spot for migrating birds. In total, 298 unique species have been recorded at the park, with the majority being seen during peak migrations in the spring and fall. The park is host to the Tawas Point Birding Festival, a three-day festival held in May that includes birding seminars and guided field trips. It is reported that it is not uncommon to see upward of 175 species of birds during a weekend visit in the spring.

Location:
Tawas Point State Park near East
Tawas, Iosco County

Coordinates:
44°15'13.7"N, 83°26'55.8"W

Tower Height:
67 feet

Recorded Bird Species:
298

Visitor Information:
www.michigan.gov/tawaslighthouse

Prothonotary warbler (*Protonotaria citrea*)

Cape May warbler (*Setophaga tigrine*)

Snowy owl (*Bubo scandiacus*)

Black-throated blue warbler (*Setophaga caerulescens*)

Eastern phoebe (*Sayornis phoebe*)

American goldfinch (*Spinus tristis*)

Common yellowthroat (*Geothlypis trichas*)

Baltimore oriole (*Icterus galbula*)

Alpena Lighthouse

Affectionately known as Little Red by some, Sputnik by others, the diminutive lighthouse that marks the entrance to Thunder Bay River has been shining since it was first lit in 1914. The first beacon at this location, the 44-foot, timber-framed structure went into operation in 1877 but in 1888 was destroyed by a fire that started at a nearby sawmill. The tower was rebuilt as a taller beacon and lit on October 1, 1888.

By 1914, the elements had taken their toll. A new concrete pier was established, topped by a four-legged skeletal steel tower. The tower was given a coat of black paint, and the new Alpena light was lit for service on the night of June 26, 1914. In the 1950s, the tower was painted red to increase its visibility during the day. After the Russian satellite Sputnik was launched in October 1957, people noticed the striking similarities between the two, resulting in many referring to the light as Sputnik. These days it's more common to hear the light lovingly called Little Red.

One doesn't have to go far from the light for good birdwatching opportunities, since it sits near the entrance to the Alpena Marina, a popular spot for gulls and waterfowl. A little over 2 miles upriver is the 500-acre Alpena wildlife sanctuary, comprising sections of Thunder Bay River and its islands. Great birding opportunities can be found both on the water and in Alpena's Duck Park and Island Park. The sanctuary and parks have a recorded combined count of 131 bird species, with high counts of waterfowl and passerines.

About 4 miles to the northeast of Little Red is another birding hotspot: Isaacson Bay, which lies within the boundaries of the Audubon's state-level North Point Important Bird Area. This shallow bay is interspersed with wetlands, which, depending on lake levels, become mudflats that are excellent for spotting shorebirds. Isaacson Bay has a recorded species count of 162, with high counts of gulls, waterfowl, and shorebirds. Five miles south of the light is another birding hotspot at Partridge Point. With a mix of forest, wetland, and Lake Huron shoreline, Partridge Point has a recorded species count of 110.

Location:
Mouth of Thunder Bay River, Alpena

Coordinates:
45°3'37.5"N, 83°25'22.44"W

Tower Height:
34 feet

Visitor Information:
www.alpenalighthouse.org

Osprey (*Pandion haliaetus*)

Trumpeter swan (*Cygnus buccinator*)

Mute swan (*Cygnus olor*)

Green heron (*Butorides virescens*)

Black-throated green warbler (*Setophaga virens*)

Eastern bluebird (*Sialia sialis*)

Yellow warbler (*Setophaga petechia*)

Wood duck (*Aix sponsa*)

Charity Island Lighthouse

Big Charity Island, a 222-acre island in Michigan's Saginaw Bay, is surrounded by dangerous shoals. To warn sailors of the danger, Congress appropriated funds for a lighthouse on the north end of the island in 1856. Construction of the 45-foot-tall light and keeper's dwellings began soon after, and the light became operable in 1857.

By 1939, after the construction of an updated lighthouse on nearby Gravelly Shoal, Charity Island Lighthouse was decommissioned and its light extinguished. Abandoned by the United States Coast Guard (USCG) and left at the mercy of the elements, the station began to deteriorate. In 1987, the USCG deemed the property excess and sold the island to a private entity in 1992. The lighthouse and grounds are now privately owned and can be visited through a private charter from the mainland out of Au Gres or Caseville, Michigan.

Today, all that remains of the original lighthouse station is the tower, though a replica keeper's dwelling was constructed. Since 1997, most of the island belongs to the US Fish and Wildlife Service and is part of the Michigan Islands National Wildlife Preserve. This ecologically sensitive area is off-limits to the public.

Saginaw Bay, including Charity Islands, is considered an Important Bird Area by the Audubon Society. Big Charity Island, its sister island (Little Charity Island), and the shoals in Saginaw Bay provide a stopover for migrating birds, as well as breeding and wintering grounds. One of the earliest recorded birding expeditions to the island was made in 1910 by a University of Michigan Museum group, which documented 162 bird species. A second expedition the following year added eight more species to the list.

Location:
34 miles from the mouth of the Saginaw River

Coordinates:
44°01'53"N, 83°26'08"W

Tower Height:
45 feet

Recorded Bird Species:
200+

Visitor Information:
www.charityisland.net

Brown thrasher (*Toxostoma rufum*) fledgling

Ring-billed gull (*Larus delawarensis*)

Barn swallow (*Hirundo rustica*)

Eastern kingbird (*Tyrannus tyrannus*)

Northern flicker (*Colaptes auratus*)

Eastern wood-pewee (*Contopus virens*)

Willow flycatcher (*Empidonax traillii*)

Yellow warbler (*Setophaga petechia*)

Old Presque Isle Lighthouse

Presque Isle Peninsula extends from Lake Huron's shore between the cities of Alpena and Rogers City. The name, given by seventeenth-century French fur traders, is derived from the French *presqu'île*, meaning "almost an island"— a fitting moniker since most of the peninsula is attached to the mainland by a narrow strip of land. The Presque Isle Peninsula helps form Presque Isle Harbor to the south and the aptly named North Bay to the north, both of which provide much-needed shelter from the fury of Lake Huron storms.

This peninsula is special because it is home to two lighthouses and a set of range lights, all within a mile of each other. The Old Presque Isle Lighthouse that sits at the entrance to the Presque Isle Harbor on the south end of the peninsula was commissioned in 1838, constructed in 1839, and lit in September 1840. It shone bright for nearly thirty years before the US Lighthouse Board determined that its height and position made it valuable only as a harbor light. The board commissioned a set of range lights to guide mariners into the harbor, and a new coastal light to be erected on the north end of the peninsula. With the lighting of the New Presque Isle Lighthouse in 1871, the old beacon was deemed obsolete and its light extinguished.

The lighthouse tower and structures sat abandoned until 1897, when they were purchased by a private owner through public auction. The property changed owners a few more times and opened as a museum in 1940. In 1992, because of increasing taxes and insurance costs, the owner sold the property to the state of Michigan to become part of an existing state park, and donated the structures to the township. Today the light still operates as a museum maintained by the Presque Isle Township Museum Society.

The lighthouse grounds are open during museum hours. The harbor is a hotspot for waterfowl, gulls, and passerines, with high counts of American redstart.

Location:
Presque Isle Township

Coordinates:
45°20'31.3"N, 83°28'41.8"W

Tower Height:
38 feet

Visitor Information:
www.presqueislelighthouses.org

American redstart (*Setophaga ruticilla*)

Black-throated blue warbler (*Setophaga caerulescens*)

Blue-headed vireo (*Vireo solitarius*)

Bald eagle (*Haliaeetus leucocephalus*)

Horned grebe (*Podiceps auratus*)

Great egret (*Ardea alba*)

Rose-breasted grosbeak (*Pheucticus ludovicianus*)

New Presque Isle Lighthouse

When the US Lighthouse Board decided to replace the Old Presque Isle Lighthouse with a new beacon on the northern shore of the peninsula, district engineer Orlando M. Poe drew up plans for the new station, the first in a string of Great Lakes lighthouses he designed. His vision called for a classic but elegantly ornate tower rising to an astounding 109 feet. The board approved the plan in 1869, and the light was lit at the beginning of the shipping season in 1871.

Poe's new design was so successful that it would be reused many times for future Great Lakes light stations, including Au Sable Point light on Lake Superior and Big Sable Point and Little Sable Point lights on Lake Michigan. The New Presque Isle Lighthouse was manned for nearly one hundred years until 1970, when the light was automated and the stations abandoned. The property was leased to the county in the 1980s as a county park, and by 1998 the US Coast Guard transferred the land to the county permanently. The Presque Isle Township Museum Society was formed to preserve the station for future generations.

Today, the tower is open for climbing in the New Presque Isle Lighthouse Park, during hours established by the Presque Isle Township Museum Society. Birding opportunities in the 99-acre park abound. The area consists of vast tracts of cedar, balsam, and birch forest and long stretches of unspoiled Lake Huron shoreline. A walk along any of the trails leading to the shore turns up a variety of woodpeckers and passerines. Shorebirds have been reported in decent numbers along the beaches, and high numbers of waterfowl can be seen floating offshore during migrations.

Leaving the peninsula, a short, 10-mile drive will bring you to Thompson Harbor State Park, which boasts a reported 142 species of birds. This 5,000-acre undeveloped park is accessible with the purchase of a state recreational pass and features many nature trails and over 7 miles of Lake Huron shoreline.

Location:
Presque Isle Township

Coordinates:
45°21'23.259"N, 83°29'32.37"W

Tower Height:
109 feet

Visitor Information:
www.presqueislelighthouses.org

American redstart (*Setophaga ruticilla*)

Blue-gray gnatcatcher (*Polioptila caerulea*)

Courting trumpeter swans (*Cygnus buccinator*)

Brown thrasher (*Toxostoma rufum*)

Mourning dove (*Zenaida macroura*)

Eastern wood-pewee (*Contopus virens*)

Swainson's thrush (*Catharus ustulatus*)

Sandhill crane (*Grus canadensis*)

Round Island Lighthouse

The Straits of Mackinac, a narrow passage between Michigan's Upper and Lower Peninsulas that connects Lake Huron and Lake Michigan, has been an important shipping lane for centuries. Native American tribes converged on the straits for millennia to take advantage of its natural bounty, and they considered the islands sacred burial places. The seventeenth century saw the French ply these waters in search of furs to send back home, followed not long after by the British; by the end of the century, the newly formed United States of America had laid claim to the area.

With increases in lumber, iron, and copper trades during the nineteenth century, the Straits of Mackinac became a major shipping lane. As ships grew larger to carry more cargo, their drafts grew deeper, making the reefs and shoals of the Straits more dangerous. In 1894 the Round Island Lighthouse was constructed to mark the narrow passage between Mackinac Island and Round Island and warn sailors off the shoal at the island's west end.

The light was automated in 1924, eliminating the need for a keeper. With the construction of the Round Island Passage light on the opposite side of the channel in 1947, the Round Island Lighthouse was deemed obsolete and left to the mercy of the elements. During one particularly violent storm in 1972, a corner of the lighthouse collapsed, leaving the interior exposed and accessible to vandals. Worried the building would collapse, a society was formed to save and restore the light.

Today the light is owned by the US Forest Service. It has become an icon of the Straits of Mackinac, viewed by hundreds of thousands of people who ride the ferries to Mackinac Island annually. The Round Island Lighthouse Preservation Society offers tours once a year, if safe public transportation can be arranged.

The Audubon Society named the Straits of Mackinac a state-level Important Bird Area. High concentrations of raptors travel through this natural funnel during spring and fall migrations. Pointe LaBarbe, on the northern shore of Lake Michigan west of the Mackinac Bridge, boasts an impressive 228 reported bird species, followed closely by Mackinac Island to the east in Lake Huron, with 188 species.

Location:
Round Island, Mackinac County

Coordinates:
45°50'13.8"N, 84°36'59.7"W

Tower Height:
57 feet

Visitor Information:
www.roundislandlightmichigan.com

Red-eyed vireo (*Vireo olivaceus*)

Canada goose (*Branta canadensis*)

Hooded merganser (*Lophodytes cucullatus*)

White-crowned sparrow (*Zonotrichia leucophrys*)

Cape May warbler (*Setophaga tigrina*)

Dark-eyed junco (*Junco hyemalis*)

Hermit thrush (*Catharus guttatus*)

Green heron (*Butorides virescens*)

Sturgeon Point Lighthouse

Sturgeon Point Lighthouse sits on a natural point approximately halfway between Tawas Point Lighthouse and the lighthouse on Thunder Bay Island, off Alpena, Michigan. In 1866 the United States Lighthouse Board requested funding for a light to mark the shallow reef that extends a mile and a half from the point. Congress agreed, and the funds were granted in March 1867.

The 60 acres encompassing the point were purchased from a local landowner, and plans for construction were completed and approved by July 1868. The lighthouse was to open for the 1869 shipping season, and a local fisherman was appointed as the station's first keeper. However, he failed to report for duty until November. By then, it was deemed too late in the season to light the tower. Notice went out that the light would be lit for the beginning of the 1870 shipping season.

By 1913, a then-recent invention of a solar valve for acetylene lamps allowed the Lighthouse Board to experiment with automating the Sturgeon Point light, making it the second light on the Great Lakes, behind Charity Island, to be automated. By 1939, electric lines were run to the station, and the lamp was replaced with an electric light. By 1941, the last crew left. In 1982 the light was leased to the Alcona Historical Society, and restoration followed soon after. Today the station is a maritime museum.

This lighthouse offers some good birding opportunities, since it sits inside Sturgeon Point State Park. A total of 153 bird species have been reported on its 76 acres, which consist of white cedar, white pine, and birch forests; marshland; and a stretch of Lake Huron shoreline. Waterfowl such as red-breasted mergansers have been reported offshore in high numbers, while the forests are good for spotting woodpeckers.

Blue jays, cedar waxwing, pine sisken, and snow bunting have also been reported in high numbers. During spring migrations, warblers can be found happily flitting through the trees, while various shorebirds hang out along the shoreline. Reported rarities include snowy owls, long-eared owls, and piping plovers.

Location:
3 miles north of Harrisville

Coordinates:
44°42'45.7"N, 83°16'21.8"W

Tower Height:
71 feet

Visitor Information:
www.alconahistoricalsociety.com

Blue jay (*Cyanocitta cristata*)

Barred owl (*Strix varia*)

Eastern screech owl (*Megascops asio*)

Killdeer (*Charadrius vociferous*) fledgling

Downy woodpecker (*Picoides pubescens*)

Yellow warbler (*Setophaga petechia*)

Cedar waxwing (*Bombycilla cedrorum*)

Forty Mile Point Lighthouse

By the late 1800s, the United States Lighthouse Board decided a series of coastal lights were needed to fill the gaps between existing stations. The idea was that a ship at sea should always be within sight of a lighthouse. For approximately 13 miles of a 50-mile stretch of coastline between the light on the Presque Isle peninsula and the crib light at the entrance to the Cheboygan River, mariners were out of range of a visible light. In 1890, the Lighthouse Board requested funds to establish a lighthouse at Hammond Bay, halfway between the two established lights.

Congress authorized the project in 1893 but failed to provide construction funding until August 1894. Property near the southern end of Hammond Bay was purchased, and construction of the Forty Mile Point light finally began in July 1896. Construction was completed by November of that year, keepers were appointed, and the Forty Mile Point light was exhibited for the first time in May 1897.

The light was automated in 1969, and by 1971 the land surrounding the lighthouse was taken over by Presque Isle County to become a public park, with the Coast Guard retaining ownership of the light. When the government declared the Forty Mile Point Lighthouse surplus in 1996, Presque Isle County and the Forty Mile Point Lighthouse Society applied to take ownership. Once the application was approved in 1998, restoration and preservation efforts began in earnest. Today, the lighthouse and grounds are open to the public as a nautical museum.

The park is a mix of Lake Huron shoreline and white cedar forest. Many varieties of waterfowl can be seen off the shore, and warblers, such as American redstart, can be found in high numbers in the forested area, among other species. About 6 miles north of the light sits Hammond Bay Biological Station, with ninety species of birds reported, and the Herman Vogler Conservation Area lies 5 miles to the south, with one hundred species reported.

Location:
7 miles northwest of Rogers City

Coordinates:
45°29'12"N, 83°54'48"W

Tower Height:
52 feet

Visitor Information:
www.40milepointlighthouse.org

American redstart (*Setophaga ruticilla*)

Black-throated green warbler (*Setophaga virens*)

American goldfinch (*Spinus tristis*)

American robins (*Turdus migratorius*)

Black-capped chickadee (*Poecile atricapillus*)

Northern parula (*Setophaga americana*)

Rose-breasted grosbeak (*Pheucticus ludovicianus*)

Lake Michigan

Point Betsie Lighthouse

Ships sailing between ports in southern Lake Michigan and the Straits of Mackinac take advantage of a natural channel known as the Manitou Passage, located between the Manitou islands, the Beaver Island archipelago, and the mainland. In the early 1800s, ships traveling north would begin their turn into the passage when they saw a natural point on the mainland approximately 20 miles south of South Manitou Island, then known as Point Betsey. By 1853, Congress appropriated the funds for the construction of a lighthouse at this location to better mark the entry.

Construction of Point Betsie Lighthouse began in 1854, but, for reasons unknown, it was not completed until late 1858. Once done, a keeper was appointed, and the lamp was first lit in time for the start of the 1859 shipping season. Over the years, shifting sands, erosion, and the crushing force of ice posed a threat to the lighthouse, given its location on one of Lake Michigan's many sand dunes and proximity to the shoreline. A timber protection at the base of the dune was installed and reinforced with concrete.

Today, Benzie County owns the Point Betsie Lighthouse, which it acquired from the US Bureau of Land Management in 2004. The facility is maintained by the nonprofit Friends of Point Betsie Lighthouse and is open to the public during the summer. The light remains an active aid to navigation for ships traveling through the Manitou Passage.

Adjacent to the lighthouse is the Zetterberg Preserve, maintained by the Nature Conservancy. This 100-acre preserve consists of sandy beach, dunes, interdunal wetlands, and boreal forest. Cedar waxwing can often be spotted flitting around in the forested sections, while sandpipers and plovers inhabit the sandier areas. The shoreline is part of the Audubon Society's globally important Lake Michigan Long-Tailed Duck Important Bird Area, and an ideal spot for viewing waterfowl. High numbers of long-tailed duck and common loon have been reported passing the point, along with more-common waterfowl.

Location:
5 miles north of Frankfort

Coordinates:
46°46'14"N, 84°57'24"W

Tower Height:
36 feet

Visitor Information:
www.pointbetsie.org

Brown thrasher (*Toxostoma rufum*)

Black-capped chickadee (*Poecile atricapillus*)

Northern parula (*Setophaga americana*)

Barn swallow (*Hirundo rustica*)

Eastern phoebe (*Sayornis phoebe*)

Scarlet tanager (*Piranga olivacea*)

Yellow warbler (*Setophaga petechia*)

White-crowned sparrow (*Zonotrichia leucophrys*)

Peninsula Point Lighthouse

Stonington Peninsula lies east of Escanaba, in Michigan's Upper Peninsula. This landmass juts south into Lake Michigan, helping form the natural harbors of Big Bay de Noc to the east and Little Bay de Noc to the west. At the southernmost point sits what remains of Peninsula Point Lighthouse.

Prior to its lighting in 1865, mariners had to take great caution when navigating to Escanaba in the dark of night to avoid grounding on shoals that extended between the point and St. Martin's Island. The one-and-a-half-story keeper's dwelling and attached 40-foot square tower warned mariners of the danger until the 1930s, when, due to advances in ship-building and the increase in size of these newer ships, the shipping lanes moved farther out into the lake. By 1934 the Minneapolis Shoal light was completed, and Peninsula Point Lighthouse was decommissioned within two years. The US Forest Service took ownership of the lighthouse in 1937, and the Civilian Conservation Corps was tasked with repairing the buildings and installing picnic grounds.

Lacking funds to maintain the lighthouse, in 1948 the US Forest Service considered demolishing the structure. Fortunately, the Stonington Grange (of the National Grange of the Order of Patrons of Husbandry) agreed to take on the task. Their restoration efforts were successful, earning them first prize in a statewide Grange Community Service contest in 1949. Sadly, the keeper's dwelling burned in 1959, leaving only the tower remaining. Today it is part of the Hiawatha National Forest. The glass and doors have been removed, allowing public access for climbing the tower for a view of Lake Michigan.

Peninsula Point is an excellent birding hotspot, with 250 bird species recorded, many of which have been reported in high numbers. Bird enthusiasts have compared the activity here to that of Canada's Point Pelee, known for its excellent migration activity. It has even seen its share of "fallout" when storms force high concentrations of migrating birds to land. As if the lighthouse and excellent birding weren't enough, in late August and early September thousands of migrating monarch butterflies rest on the point before continuing their journey to Mexico.

Location:
Stonington Peninsula, Delta County

Coordinates:
45°40'5.52"N, 86°57'59.76"W

Tower Height:
40 feet

Semipalmated plover (*Charadrius semipalmatus*)

Dunlin (*Calidris alpina*)

Black-capped chickadee (*Poecile atricapillus*)

American woodcock (*Scolopax minor*)

Scarlet tanager (*Piranga olivacea*)

White-throated sparrow (*Zonotrichia albicollis*)

Chestnut-sided warbler (*Setophaga pensylvanica*)

Cape May warbler (*Setophaga tigrina*)

Magnolia warbler (*Setophaga magnolia*)

Big Sable Point Lighthouse

The area once aptly called Grand Pointe au Sable (Great Sand Point) is known today by its modernized name, Big Sable Point. Just north of Ludington, Michigan, Big Sable Point is a natural formation of grass-covered sand dunes extending into Lake Michigan. In 1865, the United States Lighthouse Board recommended the construction of a lighthouse on the point. The US Congress agreed and granted an appropriation the following year. Construction began in early 1867, and the first light was lit later that year.

The light was electrified in 1949 and automated in 1968. Once automated, there was no longer a need for a keeper, and the buildings were abandoned, falling into disrepair. The light itself is still an active navigational aid and is now the jewel of Ludington State Park. The grounds are accessible to the public year-round. The tower and its buildings have been restored and are maintained by the Sable Points Lighthouse Keepers Association, which offers tours for a small donation during the summer.

Ludington State Park is in Mason County, which has a recorded bird count of 292 species. Roughly 5,300 acres of diverse habitat, the park is a birder's paradise. Its miles of Lake Michigan beach and sand dunes are part of the Audubon Society's Lake Michigan Long-Tailed Duck Globally Important Bird Area and have been known to host nesting pairs of piping plovers. The park's extensive trail system is ideal for a day of birding, with hotpots located along the Big Sable River, Hamlin Lake, and the nearly 2-mile trail that leads to the lighthouse at Big Sable Point.

Migrating warblers and waterfowl can be observed during the spring and fall, and snowy owls have been reported during irruption years. Olive-sided flycatchers and prairie warblers have also been recorded nesting within the park. With Big Sable Point Lighthouse and many miles of beach, dunes, rivers, lakes, marshes, and ponds that are easily accessible from the park's trail system, Ludington State Park is a must-visit for birders and lighthouse lovers alike.

Location:
Ludington State Park

Coordinates:
44°3'27.8"N, 86°30'52"W

Tower Height:
112 feet

Visitor Information:
www.splka.org

Harlequin duck (*Histrionicus histrionicus*)

Piping plover (*Charadrius melodus*)

Ring-billed gull (*Larus delawarensis*)

White-breasted nuthatch (*Sitta carolinensis*)

Black-throated blue warbler (*Setophaga caerulescens*)

Northern cardinal (*Cardinalis cardinalis*)

Gray catbird (*Dumetella carolinensis*)

St. Joseph Pier Lights

A pair of lighthouses sit on the southwestern shore of Michigan's Lower Peninsula where the 206-mile St. Joseph River empties into Lake Michigan. These are the St. Joseph Pier Lights, which mark the entrance to St. Joseph.

St. Joseph was a historically important port for shipping and transportation across Lake Michigan to Chicago during the late nineteenth and early twentieth centuries. The first federally funded lighthouse at St. Joseph was constructed in 1859 and served as the only light marking the river entrance until construction on the pier lights began in 1906. The current lights, located on the north pier, were completed in 1907 and served as range lights, allowing sailing vessels far out in Lake Michigan to accurately line up with the channel entrance.

With its grass-covered dunes, miles of Lake Michigan beach, and the river mouth, this is a popular birding spot. Public access is through Tiscornia Park on the river's north side and Silver Beach County Park on the south. Both parks offer great views of the pier lights and excellent birding opportunities. Gulls, shorebirds, ducks, and other water birds are common sights here.

Accidental and casual avian visitors have also been spotted here on occasion. According to the Michigan Bird Records Committee, casual visitors are "Species that have been recorded more than three times, but 30 or fewer times, in the last 10 years, and were recorded in fewer than nine of the last 10 years." Accidental visitors consist of "Species that have been recorded three or fewer times in the last 10 years."

During irruption years, this area has been a hotspot for snowy owl sightings. Other rarities recorded here include the magnificent frigatebird, ancient murrelet, northern gannet, brown pelican, and gyrfalcon. Along with the various resident gulls, sightings of black-headed, California, glaucous-winged, Heermann's, and Sabine's gulls have been reported, along with sandwich terns.

Location:
Mouth of the St. Joseph River, St. Joseph

Coordinates:
42°06'58"N, 86°29'36"W

Outer Tower Height:
35 feet

Inner Tower Height:
57 feet

Visitor Information:
www.stjoelighthousetours.wordpress.com

Harlequin duck (*Histrionicus histrionicus*)

American coot (*Fulica americana*)

Sanderling (*Calidris alba*)

Ring-billed gull (*Larus delawarensis*)

White-breasted nuthatch (*Sitta carolinensis*)

Mourning dove (*Zenaida macroura*)

Greater yellowlegs (*Tringa melanoleuca*)

Little Sable Point Lighthouse

In the mid-nineteenth century, vast tracts of untouched forest that once covered Michigan enticed entrepreneurs to set up logging operations to feed burgeoning cities such as Chicago and New York. As lumber production increased, so did shipping operations on the Great Lakes, and with increased shipping came a greater potential for shipping accidents and loss of life.

When the schooner *Pride* grounded on Petite Pointe au Sable (Little Sand Point) in 1871, demand for the government to establish a lighthouse increased. By 1872, the US Congress appropriated funds for a new light station on 39 acres of what is today known as Little Sable Point. Construction began in 1873 and was completed by the end of the year. A crew was appointed, and the light was lit in spring 1874.

Today the tower and original 39 acres are part of the almost 3,000-acre Silver Lake State Park. The tower is maintained by the Sable Points Lighthouse Keepers Association and is accessible to the public. The park boasts almost 4 miles of Lake Michigan shoreline, large sand dunes, and mature forests. Two hundred fifty-one bird species have been recorded within Oceana County, with 144 species found inside the park. The shore is part of the Audubon Society's Lake Michigan Long-Tailed Duck Important Bird Area.

Piping plover occur along the shore in small but growing numbers. American coot, common merganser, and bufflehead have been seen in high numbers in the park, as have horned lark, blackpoll warbler, common yellowthroat, American redstart, and cedar waxwing. Many other warbler species are spotted during spring migration.

About 20 miles outside the park is Walkinshaw Wetland Preserve, a 4,500-acre swamp managed by the US Forest Service. The preserve is a good place to look for herons and bitterns, and in the fall it is a stop-over for thousands of sandhill cranes flying south for the winter.

Location:
Silver Lake State Park south of Pentwater

Coordinates:
43°39'6"N, 86°32'20"W

Tower Height:
107 feet

Visitor Information:
www.splka.org

Blackpoll warbler (*Setophaga striata*)

Green heron (*Butorides virescens*)

Red-tailed hawk (*Buteo jamaicensis*)

Northern cardinal (*Cardinalis cardinalis*)

Sandhill cranes (*Grus canadensis*) with colt

Ruby-crowned kinglet (*Regulus calendula*)

Lake Superior

Grand Island East Channel Lighthouse

Built to guide mariners into the safe harbor of Grand Island's south shore, Grand Island East Channel Lighthouse was first lit in August 1868. The tower and dwelling structure are unique in that, even though the plans used to construct them were like other "schoolhouse"-style lights, they were built of wood instead of the standard brick. While this made for a picturesque lighthouse, it was prone to deterioration. By 1905, its condition had declined and its usefulness had diminished. A set of range lights were commissioned to replace the aging structure.

In 1908, the new range lights were lit, and the Grand Island East Channel light was decommissioned, abandoned, and left to the mercy of the elements. In 1915, the land on which the light stood was sold to a group of individuals. This peculiar situation protected the lighthouse from being removed, since no single owner had the authority to remove it. Conversely, however, no single person could maintain it either. In the years that followed, its paint peeled, exposing the bare wood; the cribs that protected the structure began to disintegrate; and the bay waters threatened to take the foundation.

A group of locals, concerned with the plight of the lighthouse, formed the East Channel Lights Rescue Project. Through fundraising efforts and with the help of the American Lighthouse Foundation, they raised enough money to rebuild the protective breakwall and begin efforts to restore the structure. Thanks to their work, this unique lighthouse still stands and has become one of the most photographed lighthouses on the Great Lakes. During summer, daily cruises such as Pictured Rocks Cruises, Glass Bottom Shipwreck Tours, and Riptide Ride feature the light.

Birdwatching opportunities are numerous. From the National Recreation Land of Grand Island itself to Pictured Rocks National lakeshore, there are many miles of trail systems open to the public. Sand Point Marsh Trail, part of the national lakeshore, boasts a reported 141 species. Closer to the town of Munising, the mouth of the Anna River is another hotspot, with 135 species reported. About 11 miles west of Munising is the mouth of the Au Train River, with a reported species number of 158 and high counts of waterfowl, shorebirds, and passerines.

Location:
Grand Island, Munising

Coordinates:
46°27'23.8"N, 86°37'22.8"W

Tower Height:
45 feet

Common yellowthroat (*Geothlypis trichas*)

Dark-eyed junco (*Junco hyemalis*)

Northern waterthrush (*Parkesia noveboracensis*)

White-breasted nuthatch (*Sitta carolinensis*)

Piping plover (*Charadrius melodus*)

Wilson's snipe (*Gallinago delicata*)

Swamp sparrow (*Melospiza georgiana*)

Mallard (*Anas platyrhynchos*)

Harlequin duck (*Histrionicus histrionicus*)

Big Bay Point Lighthouse

Big Bay Point Lighthouse stands on a roughly 40-foot cliff on a point off the shore of Lake Superior, about 30 miles northwest of Marquette. Lit in 1896, Big Bay Point light filled a gap between beacons on Huron Island and Granite Island. Consisting of a two-story, eighteen-room brick duplex that housed the keeper and his assistants, this light is similar in design to the Forty-Mile Point Light. The 64-foot tower rises from the center of the building, which, including the height of the cliff that it rests on, puts the light a little over 100 feet above Lake Superior.

The station was fully manned until 1941, when the US Coast Guard automated the light, and the assistant keeper's dwelling was rented out as a family residence. In 1951, the station was leased to the US Army to serve as an antiaircraft training facility. Large-caliber weapons were mounted on the cliff, and aircraft were towed above the lake to be used for target practice. By 1961 the lighthouse had been abandoned for almost six years and was in disrepair. The light and surrounding acreage were sold to a private owner who restored the structures for use as a summer home.

In 1979, the lighthouse changed ownership again, purchased by a small corporation that opened the station as a bed and breakfast in 1986. Adjoining lands were purchased as they became available, increasing the acreage around the lighthouse to about 100 acres. In 1992, the light and about 40 acres of the land were sold to previous guests of the bed and breakfast, who did not wish to see the pristine location further developed. The bed and breakfast continued under these new owners until 2018, when the light, along with 6 adjoining acres, was sold again. The new owner continues to run Big Bay Point Lighthouse as a bed and breakfast.

With a reported seventy-six bird species, Big Bay Point Lighthouse and grounds are a great location for birding. Guests can find a variety of birds along the many trails along the shore and in the forests. Nearby hotspots include Harlow Lake, with a recorded 106 species, and Lake Independence, with forty-six species reported. The remoteness of the area should provide good birding with great solitude.

Location:
Big Bay northwest of Marquette

Coordinates:
46°50'25"N, 87°40'55"W

Tower Height:
64 feet

Visitor Information:
www.bigbaylighthouse.com

Blackburnian warbler (*Setophaga fusca*)

Black-throated green warbler (*Setophaga virens*)

White-throated sparrow (*Zonotrichia albicollis*)

Bay-breasted warbler (*Setophaga castanea*)

Black-capped chickadee (*Poecile atricapillus*)

Song sparrow (*Melospiza melodia*)

Common yellowthroat (*Geothlypis trichas*)

Au Sable Point Lighthouse

An estimated 600 shipwrecks are lying on the bottom of Lake Superior. Nearly one-third are in the waters off the lake's southern shore between Munising and Whitefish Point, known as the Shipwreck Coast. In the 1860s, mariners were forced to navigate blindly through the treacherous 80 miles between the light at Whitefish Point and Grand Island North light. Heeding the desperate calls of sailors, the US Lighthouse Board recommended adding a light in 1867. However, Congress didn't approve the funds until 1872.

A site for the new light was selected roughly 12 miles west of Grand Marais on a point between the majestic sandstone cliffs of Pictured Rocks to the west and the towering dunes of the Grand Sable Banks to the east. Construction of the Au Sable Point Lighthouse began in 1873 and finished up in August 1874.

The lighthouse was manned for more than eighty years until 1958, when the US Coast Guard automated the light, eliminating the need for a keeper. The station was boarded up and abandoned, except for the occasional visit by the Coast Guard to ensure the light was still shining. The creation of Pictured Rocks National Lakeshore in 1966 meant that the station was surrounded by a national park. Less than two years later the lighthouse was incorporated into the land and the grounds were opened to the public. Lighthouse restoration began in earnest in 1998, and it is now open for summer tours.

Those willing to trek the nearly 2-mile trail from Hurricane River Campground to the Au Sable light station are rewarded with the majestic scenery of Lake Superior's shoreline. Pictured Rocks National Lakeshore has a reported 160 species, with forty-nine from the Hurricane River Campground area alone. The trail to the lighthouse is good for spotting passerines (including warblers), especially during spring migration. Once they reach the light, visitors are rewarded with a breathtaking view of the Grand Sable dunes.

Location:
Pictured Rocks National Lakeshore

Coordinates:
46°40'23"N, 86°08'21.6"W

Tower Height:
87 feet

Ruby-crowned kinglet (*Regulus calendula*)

Blackburnian warbler (*Setophaga fusca*)

Blue jay (*Cyanocitta cristata*)

Dark-eyed junco (*Junco hyemalis*)

House wren (*Troglodytes aedon*)

Cape May warbler (*Setophaga tigrina*)

Marquette Harbor Lighthouse

With the discovery of large iron ore deposits on the Upper Peninsula in 1844, the city of Marquette became a shipping port. By 1850, Congress had recommended that a harbor light be built. A site was selected on a rocky peninsula between the harbor and Presque Isle peninsula on the bay's western shore. Construction commenced in 1852, and the new beacon opened for business at the beginning of the 1853 shipping season.

With shipping increasing on Lake Superior—mostly due to the opening of locks at Sault Ste. Marie—and the rapid deterioration of the original lighthouse structures, the US Lighthouse Board requested—and Congress approved—funds for a new lighthouse in 1865. Construction of the brick dwelling and attached tower commenced immediately on the highest point of the peninsula, and the station went into service in 1866. This lighthouse is still being used as a navigational aid.

In 2002, the Marquette Maritime Museum took control of the lighthouse through a thirty-year lease from the US Coast Guard, and restoration efforts began soon after. With the help of local students, floors were resurfaced and walls were patched and painted. In July 2016, the land and structures were deeded outright to the City of Marquette. Today the area is open to the public as a park; the lighthouse is an extension of the museum and is open for scheduled tours during the summer.

Birding opportunities abound, with the lower harbor sporting a reported species count of 180 birds. Roughly 3 miles north of the lighthouse is Marquette's 323-acre Presque Isle Park, with a reported 212 species. The park's many hiking trails are good for catching sight of high numbers of waterfowl and sandpipers, as well as warblers during spring migration. Just outside the park is the Presque Isle Bog Walk, a small but impressive nature preserve. Two hundred four bird species have been reported on the quarter-mile trail that winds through an urban bog, along with high concentrations of songbirds during the spring and fall migrations.

Location:
Marquette Harbor

Coordinates:
46°32'48.08"N, 87°22'33.76"W

Tower Height:
40 feet

Visitor Information:
www.mqtmaritimemuseum.com

Black-capped chickadee (*Poecile atricapillus*)

Chestnut-sided warbler (*Setophaga pensylvanica*)

Gray jay (*Perisoreus canadensis*)

Snowy owl (*Bubo scandiacus*)

Canada goose (*Branta canadensis*)

Wood duck (*Aix sponsa*)

Hairy woodpecker (*Leuconotopicus villosus*)

American robins (*Turdus migratorius*)

Whitefish Point Lighthouse

Considered one of the most important lights on Lake Superior, the Whitefish Point Lighthouse is also the oldest operating lighthouse on the lake. At the tip of Whitefish Point, it marks the entrance to Whitefish Bay, where downbound ships make the turn on their way to the lock system at Sault Ste. Marie.

In 1849, the first lighthouse, a stone tower standing 65 feet tall, was lit at this location. By 1855, when Michigan began construction on a new lock at Sault Ste. Marie, the US government, expecting an increase in shipping traffic, ordered the lighthouse updated. Appropriations for this new light were granted in 1861, and construction began on the cast-iron tower that still operates today. This new light, standing 75 feet tall, was first lit in 1862.

Still an active navigational aid, the light and grounds are also home to the Great Lakes Shipwreck Museum. The Great Lakes Shipwreck Historical Society maintains the property, which houses the lighthouse and Coast Guard buildings as a museum dedicated to preserving the history of shipping on the lakes. One of the main attractions of the museum is the ship's bell from the SS *Edmund Fitzgerald*, recovered in 1995 from the shipwreck, which lies some 17 miles northwest.

Whitefish Point is also a Globally Important Bird Area and is home to Whitefish Point Bird Observatory, a nonprofit dedicated to monitoring and documenting the birds that visit the point during spring and fall migrations. With a recorded count of 340 bird species, Whitefish Point is a birder's paradise, with tens of thousands of birds regularly witnessed. Staffed by dedicated professionals, Whitefish Point Bird Observatory makes annual raptor and waterbird counts, along with an unparalleled owl-banding effort three times a year. Northern saw-whet, boreal, long-eared, short-eared, great horned, great gray, barred, snowy, and northern hawk owls have been reported during these operations.

The grounds at Whitefish Point are open to the public, with the lighthouse, museum, and bird observatory buildings accessible during posted hours.

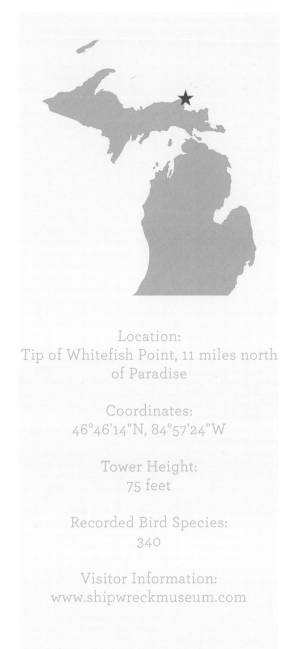

Location:
Tip of Whitefish Point, 11 miles north of Paradise

Coordinates:
46°46'14"N, 84°57'24"W

Tower Height:
75 feet

Recorded Bird Species:
340

Visitor Information:
www.shipwreckmuseum.com

Black-billed cuckoo (*Coccyzus erythropthalmus*)

Bay-breasted warbler (*Setophaga castanea*)

Red-shouldered hawk (*Buteo lineatus*) fledgling

Sanderling (*Calidris alba*)

Short-billed dowitcher (*Limnodromus griseus*)

White-crowned sparrow (*Zonotrichia leucophrys*)

Blackburnian warbler (*Setophaga fusca*)

Savannah sparrow (*Passerculus sandwichensis*)

Lake St. Clair

St. Clair Flats Range Lights

First lit in 1859, St. Clair Flats Range Lights mark the entrance to the south shipping channel through the St. Clair Flats, the largest freshwater delta in the world. Before their construction, mariners, out of fear of entering the shallow channel at night, would anchor in the aptly named Anchor Bay to wait out the darkness. The range lights allowed mariners to line up with the channel to ensure safe passage.

The lights remained in operation until 1907, when they were taken out of service, only to be reestablished in 1915. By 1921, however, most shipping traffic was using the channel that had been created in 1867, and the "old" south channel was relegated to small watercraft and tugs. The lights were discontinued again in 1934 and left to the mercy of the elements. By 1989, the cribs were all but gone and the front tower exhibited a noticeable lean. With the towers in danger of falling into the lake, the volunteer organization Save Our South Channel Lights was formed to rebuild the cribs and restore the towers for future generations to enjoy.

Since these lights are within Lake St. Clair, the best way to view them is by boat, though distant views can be had at the southern tip of Harsen's Island, in the St. Clair River. The flats and surrounding area offer many birdwatching opportunities, and gulls, terns, and waterfowl are regulars around the lights. About 5 miles west of the south channel is the Harley Ensign Memorial Boat Launch, which features a small but lovely nature trail that not only has a reported 196 species—including great horned, snowy, northern saw-whet, and long- and short-eared owls—but is known as a hotspot for the occasional accidental visitor. Not far from the boat launch, Lake St. Clair Metropark boasts an impressive 283 reported bird species. The park is a prime spot for viewing waterfowl, passerines, and shorebirds year-round.

The southern end of Harsen's Island and St. Clair Flats are considered important bird areas at the state level. The flats, nearly 25,000 acres of cattail, bulrush, grasses, and open water, create a natural nesting spot for rails, sora, moorhen, bitterns, and terns. Unusually high numbers of waterfowl have been seen here, some of the 208 species reported on the island.

Location:
Southeastern tip of Harsen's Island

Coordinates:
42°32'16.4"N, 82°41'35.4"W

Front Tower Height:
17 feet

Rear Tower Height:
40 feet

Visitor Information:
www.soschannellights.org

Piping plover (*Charadrius melodus*)

Brown thrasher (*Toxostoma rufum*)

Northern parula (*Setophaga americana*)

Ruby-throated hummingbird (*Archilochus colubris*)

Great egret (*Ardea alba*)

Red-winged blackbird (*Agelaius phoeniceus*)

Detroit River

William Livingstone Memorial Light

The William Livingstone Memorial Light is the only lighthouse tower in the nation that is constructed entirely out of marble. Located inside the boundaries of the 982-acre Belle Isle State Park, this light was erected to honor the life and works of William Livingstone, who served as president of the Lake Carriers' Association from 1902 until his death in 1925. Erected on land and donated by the City of Detroit with funds from the Lake Carriers' Association and citizens of Detroit, the beacon was first lit in 1930.

Designed in the art deco style by architect Albert Kahn and erected by sculptor Gaza Moroti, it consists of a fluted shaft of white marble that rests on an octagonal platform of stairs, also made of marble. Sitting atop the tower is the octagonal bronze and glass lantern room, whose light can be seen for 16 miles. The lighthouse is also adorned with ornamental sculptures above the bronze entrance door and at the top of each of the flutes. These features make the William Livingstone Memorial Light a truly one-of-a-kind lighthouse.

Belle Isle is also a great birding spot, with a count of 249 species recorded within the park. This island area consists of a mix of Detroit River shoreline, untouched grasslands, and wet-mesic forest. The island sits in the path of a migratory flyway for waterfowl, with large numbers typically witnessed in the spring and fall. Songbirds and raptors can be seen in all seasons, with spring and fall being the best times to spot migrating warblers. Belle Isle is designated as part of the Audubon Society's Detroit River Important Bird Area, recognized for outstanding concentrations of wintering and migrating waterfowl.

A state park, the island is accessible by car with the purchase of a Michigan State Park Recreation pass. Apart from the lighthouse and scenic beauty, Belle Isle is home to the Dossin Great Lakes Museum—a maritime museum dedicated to Detroit's role in maritime history—and the Anna Scripps Whitcomb Conservatory—a greenhouse and botanical garden that boasts one of the largest municipally owned collections of orchids in the United States.

Location:
Belle Isle

Coordinates:
42°20'49.27"N, 82°57'15.52"W

Tower Height:
58 feet

Tufted titmouse (*Baeolophus bicolor*)

Great blue heron (*Ardea herodias*)

Cooper's hawk (*Accipiter cooperii*) with prey

Wood duck (*Aix sponsa*) pair

Prothonotary warbler (*Protonotaria citrea*)

Northern mockingbird (*Mimus polyglottos*)

References

Anderson, Kraig. "Lighthouse Friends." www.lighthousefriends.com.

Cornell Lab of Ornithology. "All about Birds." www.allaboutbirds.org.

Michigan Audubon Society. www.michiganaudubon.org.

Michigan Bird Records Committee. www.mibirdrecords.com.

National Audubon Society. www.audubon.org.

Pepper, Terry. "Seeing the Light." www.terrypepper.com.

US Fish and Wildlife Service. www.fws.gov.

US Forest Service. www.fs.fed.us.